Me, Myself, and I:

THE MORE Grammar Changes, THE MORE IT Remains the Same

by Rebecca Stefoff

WITHDRAWN

Consultant: Robert L. McConnell, PhD

CAPSTONE PRESS
a capstone imprint

Fact Finders Books are published by Capstone Press,
1710 Roe Crest Drive, North Mankato, Minnesota 56003
www.mycapstone.com

Library of Congress Cataloging-in-Publication Data
· Library of Congress Cataloging-in-Publication Data can be found on the Library of
Congress website.
978-1-5157-6387-1 (library hardcover)
978-1-5157-6392-5 (paperback)
978-1-5157-6064-5 (ebook PDF)

Editorial Credits:
Michelle Bisson, editor; Bobbie Nuytten, designer; Tracy Cummins, media researcher;
Laura Manthe, production specialist

Photo Credits:
Alamy Stock Photo: World History Archive, 12–13; Bridgeman Images: Pāṇini (colour
litho), Indian School/Dinodia, 6; Getty Images: CBS Photo Archive, 22; CORBIS/
Historical Picture Archive, 9; iStockphoto: izusek, 5; Shutterstock: Aratehortua, 25,
Beatriz Gascon J, 20, Dja65, 26, Elya Vatel, 23, Enlightened Media, 4, Fer Gregory,
7, Gang Liu, 27, Hedzun Vasyl, 18, I. Pilon, 15, JoMo333, 11, Kakmyc, 24, kstudija,
cover and interior design element, Laslo Ludrovan, 17, Late Night Rabbit, 19,
mimagephotography, 29, Photo Melon, 28, Rawpixel.com, 10, Samuel Borges
Photography, cover (left, middle, and right), Triff, 8

Printed in China.
010343F17

Table of Contents

CHAPTER ONE

Rules
and Why People Break Them

What would you say if your sister was supposed to share a banana with you, but she kept the whole banana?

1 "Hey, give some of that banana to I."

2 "You have to share that banana with me."

3 "You and me should split that banana."

4 "Half of that banana is for myself."

Which sentences sound right to you? Which ones sound wrong? (You'll find answers and explanations on page 31.) The reason some answers sound better than others has to do with **grammar**. "Me, myself, and I" is one of the grammar puzzles solved in this book. (There isn't room for more than a few.) You'll also discover how and why language and grammar keep changing.

grammar—the set of rules for how words can be used and how sentences can be made

Me, Myself, or I?

So, when you speak to your sister about that banana, should you call yourself *me, myself,* or *I*? That depends on who or what is the subject of your sentence.

The subject does the action in the sentence, such as handing over half of a banana—or refusing to hand it over. If you are the subject in the sentence (the active person), call yourself *I*. If you are mentioned in the sentence, but you're not the active person, call yourself *me*.

Here's another example: "Between you and I, this movie stinks," you say to your best friend. Who or what is the subject of that sentence? The movie is the subject! The action it is doing is stinking. You're part of the sentence, but you are not the subject. The right word to use in that sentence is *me*.

People often say *I* in the sentence on page 5 because they are afraid *me* is wrong. They worry about *me* because they have been told that a sentence such as "Jimmy and me went to the movies" is wrong. (It is. It should be "Jimmy and I went to the movies," because *Jimmy* and *I* are subjects.)

Myself has a lot of complicated rules. Even **grammarians** do not agree on how to use it. The best rule to remember is that when you are the subject of the sentence, and the sentence already has an *I* in it, you can use *myself*.

grammarian—person who studies or writes about grammar

Did You Know?

The oldest known written guides to grammar come from India and may be 2,500 years old. A man named Panini was the first person to write that a language is a system of rules. For his own language, which is called Sanskrit, Panini listed 3,959 rules!

"I am going on a hike by myself" is a fine sentence. So is "I myself saw the UFO land on our yard." But "Toby and myself ran away from the UFO" is wrong. You need to use the subject word *I* for yourself in that sentence: "Toby and I ran away."

It's Awesome! Or Is It?

Grammar changes over time. **Usage** today is often different from what it was 50 years ago, or what it will be 50 years from now.

Awesome is a word with a changing meaning. It used to mean "tremendously impressive or overwhelming." Something *awesome* inspired awe—a powerful feeling of admiration or dread. An astronaut might speak of "the awesome spectacle of the Earth as seen from space." A sea captain might recall "the awesome might of the waves that almost crushed our ship."

These days, *awesome* is also used to mean "excellent, fantastic, wonderful." If you saw Earth from space, you would probably call the view awesome—in both meanings of the word.

usage—the way people use words and make sentences when speaking or writing

Breaking the Rules

Even the best writers sometimes break the rules. Why would a writer use bad English?

Writers often make up characters who speak in ways that aren't correct. One example is Huckleberry Finn, a backwoods boy created by author Mark Twain. Huck begins his story this way:

> *You don't know about me, without you have read a book by the name* The Adventures of Tom Sawyer; *but that ain't no matter.*

If Huck had studied grammar, he would have known that *without* should be *unless*, and *ain't no matter* should be *is no matter*. But Twain wrote the way a boy like Huck would have spoken.

Did You Know?

In German, grammar usually puts the verbs (action words) at the end of the sentence. Try that with a few sentences in English to see how it sounds. (Hint: How would that in English sound?)

Even if you're not making up a character for a story, you probably have two ways of using language: **informal** and **formal**. Think of how you talk when you're hanging out with friends, and compare that with the way you write when you are taking an English test. Is there a difference?

Being with friends is informal. You might use a lot of slang, such as calling things *cool* or *epic*. You might use sentences that do not follow the rules of grammar, such as "Julia and me went to the playground" (instead of "Julia and I"). But if you were taking a test, or writing an essay, you would use formal, correct writing.

informal—easygoing, ordinary, not necessarily strictly correct

formal—carefully correct in the use of language

TRY IT OUT!

Write a few sentences about the same place in two ways. The place could be a mansion, a neighborhood, a planet. First write about it in your best formal English, following all the rules. Then write about it in an informal way, as if you were talking to a friend. Or write about it as if you were a different character—a cowgirl, a wizard, even a cat.

CHAPTER TWO

Grammar Back Then

Treasure Island is a famous book by Robert Louis Stevenson about pirates, buried treasure—and a tricky one-legged fellow called Long John Silver. Here the hero, Jim Hawkins, tells what Silver did in one scene:

> *So saying, he stepped back a little way, till he was out of earshot, and there sat down upon a tree stump and began to whistle; spinning round now and again upon his seat so as to command a sight, sometimes of me and sometimes of the doctor, and sometimes of his unruly ruffians as they went to and fro in the sand, between the fire—which they were busy rekindling—and the house, from which they brought forth pork and bread to make the breakfast.*

Did you notice that the paragraph is one long sentence? It has a lot of **punctuation** in it too. Even though you can tell what Silver is doing, you may find the language a bit old-fashioned or hard to read.

Treasure Island was published in 1883. The way people write has changed since then. Most modern writers would use shorter sentences and not so many punctuation marks—especially in a book for young readers.

punctuation—symbols or marks placed inside sentences or between them

13

Getting the Point

If you went back far enough in time, you wouldn't find any punctuation at all.

Centuries ago, when everything was written by hand, writers just ran all the words together into one long word. Writing looked like this:

writersjustranallthewordstogetherintoonelongword

There were no breaks between words, no punctuation marks, and no capital letters to show where a new sentence started.

A lot of early writing was meant to be read out loud. To help those readers, people who copied books started putting points (dots of ink) here and there. The points showed where the reader should stop. A tiny point meant a short stop, like the pause you make when there is a comma inside a sentence. A bigger point meant a longer stop, like the pause you make between sentences.

Did You Know?

Teachers sometimes say, "Never start a sentence with *And, But,* or *However.*" But it is grammatically correct to do so. Writers of English have been doing it since at least the year 855. Grammarians didn't start complaining about it until a thousand years later.

Published in 1493, this biblical history is one of the first printed books.

Making Space

About 1,500 years ago, writers in Europe made life even easier for readers. They started to leave spaces between words. They also used bigger letters at the start of sentences. And they made more use of points, which started to look like today's commas and periods. Later they invented new punctuation, including question marks.

In the very early days, punctuation was a wild frontier. Then it was tamed by rules and order. People used more punctuation than ever around the time *Treasure Island* was written.

After about 1950, many writers started using less punctuation, especially commas. Most writers today use less punctuation than people used a hundred years ago. But good writers still must learn to handle commas, periods, and the rest of the punctuation gang.

A Thousand Years of Change

The story of a monster-hunting hero named Beowulf was first written down about 1,000 years ago. The writer used a version of English that is now called Old English. Many words changed between Old English and the English language of today. Even some letters of the Old English alphabet fell out of use. Here's the first sentence of *Beowulf* in Old English and the same sentence in modern English:

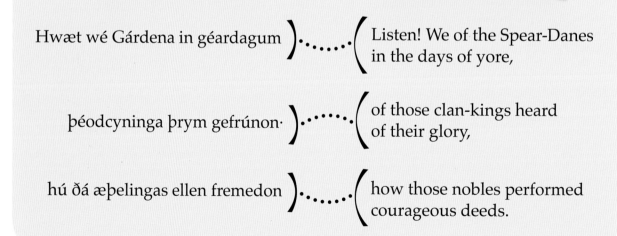

OLD ENGLISH

MODERN ENGLISH

Hwæt wé Gárdena in géardagum)......(Listen! We of the Spear-Danes in the days of yore,

þéodcyninga þrym gefrúnon·)......(of those clan-kings heard of their glory,

hú ðá æþelingas ellen fremedon)......(how those nobles performed courageous deeds.

Old-Time Grammar

Punctuation isn't the only thing that has changed over the years. Grammar used to be different too.

Seven hundred years ago, English-speaking people said *thee* and *thou* instead of "you." For "I hear you," they said, "I hear thee." For "Where are you going?" they said, "Where dost thou go?" or maybe "Where goest thou?"

Slowly, people started to say y*ou* instead of *thee* and *thou*. It took about 400 years, but by the year 1700, *thee* and *thou* were almost gone from everyday conversation.

Other things changed too. "He fighteth dragons" turned into "he fights dragons." And if the dragon-fighter was after a crown stolen from the King of Elfland? An old-time book would call it "the King's crown of Elfland." A really old book would call it "the King his crown of Elfland." What would you call it, if you wrote that story today?

CHAPTER THREE

Language Is Always Changing

You have just seen a dinosaur tied to the student bicycle rack outside your school. You think you should tell a teacher, but you don't know whose dinosaur it is. How do you say that some unknown person has left a most unusual creature among the bicycles?

You might tell the teacher that "someone left his or her dinosaur tied to the bike rack." Or "someone left his dinosaur." Or "someone left their dinosaur." A closer look at these sentences shows one way in which the English language has changed over the centuries—and is still changing.

He or She

Because you don't know whether the dinosaur belongs to a boy or a girl, you could say, "Someone left his or her dinosaur tied to the bike rack." *His* and *her* are both singular, so each word refers to just one person. You think the dinosaur belongs to one person—even if that person must be rather odd!

What about "someone left his dinosaur?" Writers used to use the male words *he, him,* and *his* for one person when they did not know whether the person was male or female. For example, the author of a ghost story in the 1900s might write, "Any stranger who saw that haunted house felt a chill in his blood."

Modern-day writers don't use *he* to stand in for *he or she.* They might say *a chill in his or her blood,* but the extra words make the sentence sound clunky. The writer could use *a chill in the blood* instead. Or "That haunted house chilled the blood of any stranger who saw it." So you would probably not say "his dinosaur."

The Word of the Year

The American Dialect Society (ADS) is a group of **linguists** who study slang and usage. Every year since 1991 they have picked a Word of the Year—something that is new, or suddenly popular.

For 1998 the Word of the Year was *e-* in front of another word to add the meaning "electronic." Examples were *e-mail* and *e-business,* which were fairly new back then.

The Word of the Year for 2006 was *plutoed.* To pluto means "to lose value or rank." Scientists had lowered Pluto from planet to minor planet. Some people then used *pluto* to say things such as "I got plutoed to a lower job at work." This Word of the Year soon *plutoed.* Millions of people, though, still use the word *email* everyday, but without the hyphen after the *e.*

linguist—scholar who studies language and how it is used

What About They?

Remember the dinosaur outside your school? What if you said to the teacher, "Someone left *their* dinosaur at the bike rack"?

They and *their* are plural. Those words refer to two or more people, who can be either male or female. If you said "*their* dinosaur," even if you thought it belonged to just one person, were you wrong?

Before the 1800s, it was common to use *they* for a single person, especially when it wasn't known whether that person was male or female. Then some grammarians decided that it was too confusing to use a plural word for one person. They started calling the usage a mistake.

Now things are going in the other direction. People are once again using the plural *they* and *their* instead of the singular *he or she* and *his or her.* Sometimes they do it by accident, because they don't understand the difference between singular and plural. Sometimes they do it on purpose, because it is an easy way to include everyone. For 2015 the American Dialect Society said that the Word of the Year was *they* used in place of *he or she.*

You're safe if you stick with *he or she.* It is always correct, and it is right for school and other formal uses. But *they* for a single person (who could be either male or female) is making a comeback in informal talk and writing.

Did You Know?

Back in the 1960s, the starship *Enterprise* on the original *Star Trek* TV show was supposed "to boldly go where no man has gone before." English teachers pointed out that it should be "to go boldly," because "to go" is a verb that should not be split by another word. People today might be more upset by "no man." Women explore space too! The show's makers would now say "no human" or "no one."

TRY IT OUT!

Write some sentences of your own with *he or she* and *his or her*. Then find another way to write the sentences without those words—or *they*. "If my brother or my sister finds out I forgot to feed the hamster, he or she will be pretty mad!" could turn into "I'm going to be in trouble if my brother or my sister finds out I forgot to feed the hamster!"

CHAPTER FOUR

The Future Is Here

The English language has always been a borrower. Many of its words started out in other languages. They were so useful that English-speakers adopted them. That's one way language can grow and change. Language is still growing—and it will keep changing in new ways.

The Burglar with Dirty Hair

A lot of English words come from Latin, the language of ancient Rome. (The ancient Romans, in turn, borrowed some of their words from the Greek language.) Many of these Latin-based words are simple, everyday things such as *circle*, which comes from the Latin word *circulus*.

German and French also gave words to English. Plenty of other languages from around the world have contributed too. If you ever see a burglar with dirty hair carrying a bag of stolen money while dressed in sleepwear, you might point out that the words *shampoo*, *loot*, and *pajamas* all come from Hindi and Urdu, two of the languages of India.

As people from around the world move to English-speaking countries, some of their words make their way into English. And English words make their way into other languages. For example, the French language doesn't have a word for *weekend*, so people in France borrowed the English word.

Did You Know?

Emoji are tiny pictures—hearts, smiley faces, cupcakes, and hundreds more—that people add to their messages on the Internet or on cellphones. People have told stories and written whole books in emoji. The Library of Congress even has an emoji version of the famous whaling novel *Moby-Dick*.

The More Things Change . . .

Language often changes when new tools are invented. One example is the printing press, a machine for making many copies of the same book.

The people of Europe started using printing presses around the year 1440. After that, more people started using punctuation and following rules of grammar. That's because with more books, more people learned to read. Writers copied the punctuation and grammar they saw in books.

The same thing is happening right now. The Internet and the cellphone are changing the way people write.

People have made up new words and slang terms to use in quick communications, such as text messages. Some, like *LOL* for "laughing out loud," save time. Other terms are names for new things, such as *app* for a program or a piece of software (an application) that is used on a computer, game console, or cellphone.

Some people have stopped using punctuation or capital letters in texts or quick messages to friends. In that way, their writing is starting to look like writing from 1,200 years ago. When writing to teachers and employers, though, correct use of language is always best!

printing press

New Language Born on the Internet

brb)·······(be right back

gr8)·······(great

idk)·······(I don't know

jk)·······(just kidding

otp)·······(favorite couple
(one true pairing)

pwned)·······(beaten (owned in
a game or contest)

omw)·······(on my way

tevs)·······(whatever

thx)·······(thanks or thank you

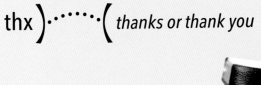

How Do New Words Get into Dictionaries?

Companies that make dictionaries have to decide what new words to add, and when to add them. Those companies pay people to spend time each day reading, in print and online. They read news articles, blogs, books, comics, and social media, such as Facebook and Twitter. When the readers come across new words (or new uses of old words), they make a note of each one. The note says how the word was used and where the reader saw it. These notes are called **citations**.

Once a word has many citations from a wide range of sources, the company adds it to the dictionary.

citation—example of usage for a word or phrase, with details of when and where it was used

...The More They Remain the Same

We know three things about the future of language.

One   Language will keep changing, just as it always has.

Two   No matter how much language changes on the surface, its deeper meaning will stay the same. It will remain a tool people use to communicate with each other and put their ideas into words.

Three   A good knowledge of how to use language will *always* be a writer's best friend.

Glossary

citation (SI-tay-shuhn)—example of usage for a word or phrase, with details of when and where it was used

formal (FOR-muhl)—carefully correct in the use of language

grammar (GRA-mer)—the set of rules for how words can be used and how sentences can be made

grammarian (GRAM-air-ee-uhn)—someone who studies or writes about grammar

informal (in-FOR-muhl)—easygoing, ordinary; not necessarily strictly correct

linguist (lin-GWIST)—scholar who studies language and how it is used

punctuation (PUNKT-chew-wgray-shuhn)—symbols or marks placed inside sentences or between them

usage (YU-sij)—the way people use words and make sentences when speaking or writing

Read More

Editors, Time for Kids. *Grammar Rules!* New York: Time for Kids, 2013.

Halverson, Jim. *Grammar Works.* Alexandria, Va.: Better Karma Publishing, 2016.

O'Conner, Patricia T. *Woe Is I Jr.: The Younger Grammarphobe's Guide to Better English in Plain English.* New York: Puffin Books, 2016.

Answers to questions on page 4:

1. Wrong. This sentence should read, "Hey, give some of that banana to me." The subject of the sentence (the person doing the action) is your sister. What the sentence really means is "You give some of that banana to me," even if you leave out the word *you*. And *I* should be *me* because the person asking for the banana is not the subject of the sentence, but *I* is a subject word.

2. Right. *You* is the subject of the sentence. When you want to refer to yourself and you're not the subject, the correct word is *me*.

3. Wrong—but people say it anyway. In this sentence, you and your sister are both subjects. You are both doing the action (splitting the banana). It is correct to use a subject word for your sister and another subject word for yourself, so the correct way to say it is, "You and I should split that banana."

4. Mostly wrong. You could say, "Half of that banana is for me," which would be completely right. If you can say *me*, there's no need to use *myself* instead. It sounds awkward. It may make people wonder whether you are using language correctly. Some writers and speakers have used *myself* this way, but it is better not to do it.

Critical Thinking Questions

1. Write down two ways that language changes over time. Then make a list of some examples of each kind of change. You can think of your own examples or use ones from this book.

2. Think of something funny or interesting that happened to you. Now, write two short paragraphs about it. For one paragraph, pretend you are writing a note to a friend your own age. For the other paragraph, pretend you are writing a paper for school or a letter to your grandparents. Are there any differences between the two paragraphs? Why or why not?

3. What is grammar? Why is it important to know how grammar works?

Internet Sites

Use FactHound to find Internet sites related to this book.

Visit *www.facthound.com*

Just type in 9781515763871 and go.

 Check out projects, games and lots more at **www.capstonekids.com**

Index